Being a Stuntman

Kathy Galashan

Published in association with The Basic Skills Agency

Hodder & Stoughton
A MEMBER OF THE HODDER HEADLINE GROUP

Acknowledgements

Cover: © Moviestore Collection

Photos: p 2 © Moviestore Collection; p 8 Moviestore Collection; p 11 Moviestore Collection; p 15 Moviestore Collection; p 17 © Moviestore Collection; p 20 FLPA/Mex; p 22 Moviestore Collection/© Disney Enterprises, Inc.; p 25 Moviestore Collection

Every effort has been made to trace copyright holders of material reproduced in this book. Any rights not acknowledged will be acknowledged in subsequent printings if notice is given to the publisher.

Orders; please contact Bookpoint Ltd, 39 Milton Park, Abingdon, Oxon OX14 4TD. Telephone: (44) 01235 400414, Fax: (44) 01235 400454. Lines are open from 9.00–6.00, Monday to Saturday, with a 24 hour message answering service.
Email address: orders@bookpoint.co.uk

British Library Cataloguing in Publication Data
A catalogue record for this title is available from the British Library

ISBN 0 340 77521 1

First published 2000
Impression number   10 9 8 7 6 5 4 3 2 1
Year   2005 2004 2003 2002 2001 2000

Typeset by GreenGate Publishing Services, Tonbridge, Kent.
Printed in Great Britain for Hodder and Stoughton Educational, a division of Hodder Headline Plc, 338 Euston Road, London NW1 3BH, by Redwood Books, Trowbridge, Wilts

Contents

1 Being a Stuntman

I'm a stuntman.
I work in films and TV.

My job is doing things
that are too dangerous
for actors to do.

I jump off buildings.
I drive through fire and into water.
I get into fights.
I crash cars and motorbikes.
I get set alight.

Sometimes it's quite easy
like riding a horse
and jumping over things.
Sometimes it is dangerous, difficult
and very uncomfortable.

That's my job as a stuntman.

A stuntman in action

People may think I'm crazy
but I'm not.
I'm very, very careful
and I think very hard
about everything I do.

Anyone can do a stunt once.
The clever bit is doing it
over and over again.
I take risks
but I think about them.
I make my job as safe as I can.

There is one thing that is difficult.
It is saying 'no'
when you think
something is too dangerous.

It's hard to say,
'No I'm not doing that,
it's not safe enough.'
But sometimes I have to.

It's OK now because I know my job
but it was hard when I started.

2 Why be a Stuntman?

When I was young,
I didn't like school.
I was no good at exams
but I loved sport
and I was good at it.
I loved a challenge.

When I left school,
I trained hard
at what I was good at.
I worked at sport
and I worked at being an actor.

I found a job
where I can use my skills.
I still enjoy a challenge
and there are plenty of those.
My timing is good.
I've learned what looks good
on the screen
and I do my job well.

3 Being an Actor

It's very important to be able to act.
A stuntman is an actor
and you have to understand
how to play to the camera.

You learn moves,
a bit like a dance.
Then you have to act
when you're told.

You don't have to be
the best driver, fighter
or horse rider in the world.

But you do have to be
good enough for the job.
Timing is very important
and you need to think clearly.

4 Setting up a Stunt

I'm a stunt co-ordinator
as well as a stuntman.

I set up a stunt
and make sure it is safe.
The director tells me what he wants
and I work out how to do it.

I sort out pay as well.
Money is always important.
I try to get the right money for the right job.

5 A Fall

Have you seen *Lethal Weapon*?
In it there is a two-man fall.
Mel Gibson and the bad guy
jump off the roof from 70 foot up.
They both fall down.

I've done a fall like that
and made it safe.
There is an air bag on the ground.
The bag has to be just right,
not too hard or too soft,
or you can hurt yourself.

A two-man fall in *The Long Kiss Goodnight*

There is practice first.
I practised from 10 foot
then 20 foot
then 30 foot
until I felt sure it was OK.

Each fall has to be safe
and it has to look good.
If the director doesn't like it
you do it again.
Sometimes I do the same stunt
five times or more.

6 A Fire Stunt

In a fire stunt real fire is used.
It's hot, very very hot.
When a stunt person is covered in fire
it's called a full burn.
A partial burn is
when only part of the person is covered.

If I don't set up the stunt right
I could get hurt.
I have to protect myself
and cover every inch of skin.

A fire stunt can be dangerous

First I put on talcum powder
to absorb the sweat.
Then I wear fireproof underwear and socks.
I put on a fire suit
and then clothes on top.
Remember I have to look like the actor.

I put a gel on my skin
that keeps the fire off for a short time.
Sometimes I wear a fireproof mask.

Imagine being covered in fire.
It's a horrible job,
very uncomfortable
and very dangerous.
When the fire is around my head
I can't breathe.
The air is too hot.

If it doesn't look right,
I have to do it all over again.

7 The Car Chase

When I plan a car chase
everyone in the chase
practises with toy cars first.
I go over and over it
so everyone knows what to do.

It is really important
to know where to put the cameras.
We have cameras inside the car,
on the front of the car
and alongside.

A ten minute car chase
can take a week to film.
It is shot from different angles.
Then it is put together
and edited afterwards.

A car chase stunt

A very dangerous stunt
is driving into water.
It's pitch black.
The windscreen can break
and you can be knocked out.
But it can be made safe.

There may be an oxygen tank
with mouthpieces in different places.
There may be bars to smash your way
out of trouble.
You have to be a really good diver
for this stunt.
It takes a lot of planning and setting up.

A dangerous stunt

8 Qualifications

In America there are stunt schools
and men and women learn
how to do stunts.
They often work in one area.
They may be a diver or a martial arts expert.

In the UK it's different.
Stunt people need to have many skills.
You need an Equity card.

Equity is the actors union
and you can join
when you get a job in entertainment.
Getting the first job
can be a problem.

I worked as an entertainer
and sports co-ordinator
in a holiday camp.
That's how I got my card.

Equity has a long list of qualifications
that you need
before you can start work
as a stuntman.
You need to have
at least six certificates at an advanced level
in different sports.

The list includes: boxing,
                   swimming,
                   driving,
                   motocross,
                   parachuting,
                   gymnastics.
Also all the martial arts like karate and lots more.

A stuntman needs qualifications in many sports

First you get a card
and your certificates.
Then you write
to the stunt committee of Equity.
They check you out and if it's OK,
you are on the books.
But you still have to get a job.

To begin with you work
with an experienced stuntman.
After three years
you can work on your own.
That's if you've had enough experience.

There are about 300 stunt people in the UK.
About 50 or 60 earn a living
as a stunt person.
Perhaps 30 make a good living.

Working with an experienced stuntman.
© Disney Enterprises, Inc.

9 The Best and the Worst

I feel good when a job has gone well.
It can be difficult and dangerous
but I feel proud of myself
when it all comes together.

I like helping new stunt people.
I pass on what I know
and make it safe for them.

Also the money can be good.
I can earn a lot of money
for a difficult stunt.
It depends how dangerous it is.

What I hate about the job
is the waiting.
Waiting to do a big stunt
is really hard.
I can be ready at 7am
and then wait until 7pm before I start.
That's when the money
doesn't seem worth it.

Also one can get hurt
and I've had the odd bang.
Luckily I've never hurt myself seriously.
I've collected a few scars
on my face and neck.
But I'd say the job is safe in Britain.
It's much safer than in America.

Every shot is planned carefully to avoid injury to the stuntman

Is it a good job?
Well what do you think?
I earn good money,
I enjoy my job a lot of the time.
I'm still alive.
Yes I'm lucky
but I'm also very careful.

10 Finding Out More

There are other *Livewire* books that tell you about some of the things in this book.

Being an Actor. This tells you how to start in acting.

Other books tell you about some of the sports mentioned.

To find out more about stunt acting write to:

British Actors Equity Association
Guild House
Upper St Martins Lane
London
WC2H 9EG

Glossary of Terms Used

Stunt a dangerous act.

Stunt person someone who does dangerous acts.

Stunt co-ordinator someone who organises and is responsible for dangerous acts.

Stunt committee a group of people who decide if one can be a stunt person. It is part of the actors union.

Contract an agreement that deals with pay and conditions of work.

Director the person in charge of the film.

Equity the union for actors.

Martial arts fighting sports like karate, kick boxing, kung fu.

Gel a jelly or cream to put on your skin.